YOU KNOW YOU'RE A CHILD OF THE 2000s WHEN...

Charlie Ellis

summersdale

YOU KNOW YOU'RE A CHILD OF THE 2000s WHEN...

Summersdale Publishers Ltd
46 West Street
Chichester
West Sussex
PO19 1RP
UK

www.summersdale.com

Printed and bound in China

ISBN: 978-1-78685-077-5

Substantial discounts on bulk quantities of Summersdale books are available to corporations, professional associations and other organisations. For details contact general enquiries: telephone: +44 (0) 1243 771107, fax: +44 (0) 1243 786300 or email: enquiries@summersdale.com.

To...

From..

Bratz dolls

Oh. Em. Gee. Barbie suddenly looked ancient next to these bobble-headed fashionistas. Dad might not have approved of all the make-up they were wearing, but we knew they were the *coolest*.

Heelys

We always knew that walking was for losers and Heelys just proved it! So we knocked down a few people on the way – we still got there faster!

BEYBLADES

At the time we thought these bad boys were the flashiest, most cutting-edge toys on the market. Looking back, it was basically a spinning top with a bit of extra plastic tacked on. Oh well, it was fun trying to fight them.

YOU KNOW YOU'RE A CHILD OF THE 2000s WHEN...

You've always thought the first mum from *My Parents Are Aliens* was better.

You still can't wear beanie hats because you're scared of looking like Craig David.

When anyone uses the phrase 'It wasn't me' you break out into a full Shaggy impersonation.

Between listening to Busted and Fountains of Wayne, you developed a bit of a thing for the older woman.

QUIZ

ONLY A CHILD OF THE 2000s WILL KNOW...

1 *Twilight* thrilled both teen and adult hearts in the noughties. When was it first published?

2 Who was the author of *Stormbreaker*, the first of the *Alex Rider* series?

3 What were the three Deathly Hallows in the final Harry Potter book, *Harry Potter and the Deathly Hallows*?

4 What did the Gruffalo encounter in the deep dark woods?

5 *Northern Lights*, *The Subtle Knife* and *The Amber Spyglass* are the names of the books in which trilogy?

6 In *How I Live Now* the main character was known as Daisy, but what was her real name?

7 Malorie Blackman wrote which critically acclaimed series of young adult novels?

8 In what year was *The Curious Incident of the Dog in the Night-Time* published?

YOU KNOW YOU'RE A CHILD OF THE 2000s WHEN...

The most embarrassing moment of your life was when your crush found out you had made a **Sims family** based on the two of you.

You still have copies of your
best **MSN conversations**
saved somewhere.

Your adventures with **LimeWire**
may have infected the family
computer more than once.

You think the only good **trainer** is
a massive skate trainer.

Dick and Dom in da Bungalow

Honestly, these were the most awesome grown-ups around. Rude, gunge-crazy and mega-bonkers, we could only hope we were as cool when we grew up.

The Wild Thornberrys

Wussy Darwin, wild Donnie, the legendary Nigel – oh, but we loved the Thornberrys. And we never had a go at talking to animals, à la Eliza, honest!

Jungle Run

On the one hand we desperately wanted to visit the seemingly exotic location of *Jungle Run* (studio? What studio?). On the other, there was a real possibility of being stuck in the temple for the rest of our lives! Dilemmas, dilemmas.

Cavegirl

Was it just us or was *Cavegirl* a bit... racy? We're no historical experts (despite all the *Horrible Histories* we read) but were there quite that many crop tops and miniskirts in prehistoric times? Who are we kidding, we were well jel of her wardrobe!

Kim Possible

Sure, there were spies, Kim kicking butt and all sorts of international shenanigans. But what was *Kim Possible* really all about? Who was the real star of the show? That would be Rufus, the naked mole-rat. Our parents were quite surprised by our Christmas list that year!

SpongeBob SquarePants

Bet you got the theme song in your head as soon as you read the title! Whether you loved good old SpongeBob sincerely or ironically, you could be sure you had the backpack, the pencil case, the T-shirt. You'd have had the SpongeBob kitchen sink if it was available.

YOU KNOW YOU'RE A CHILD OF THE 2000s WHEN...

The phrase 'Dollz Mania' sparks real excitement in you.

You're undecided on the **Hubba Bubba** vs **Bubblicious** debate.

Nothing gets you on the dance floor faster than **S Club 7**'s 'Don't Stop Movin''.

You lost more than one tooth to a big handful of strawberry **Millions**.

QUIZ

1. Who did Lennox Lewis knock out in 2002 to cement his boxing legacy?

2. In what year did England win the Rugby World Cup?

3. Which female British runner swept the 2004 Olympics, winning the 800 m and 1500 m?

4. England won the Ashes in 2005 after how many years of defeat?

5 Who was named the boxing fighter of the decade by the BWAA, WBC and WBO?

6 Zinedine Zidane infamously did what to Marco Materazzi in the 2006 World Cup?

7 Usain Bolt smashed the 100 m and 200 m world records at which Olympics?

8 Which years did Roger Federer NOT win the Wimbledon Men's Singles title?

Answers: 1. Mike Tyson **2.** 2003 **3.** Dame Kelly Holmes
4. Sixteen years **5.** Manny Pacquiao **6.** Headbutted him
7. 2008 **8.** 2000, 2001, 2002 and 2008

17

YOU KNOW YOU'RE
A CHILD OF THE
2000s
WHEN...

You're pretty sure that crimped
hair will come back into fashion
at some point soon.

You are 100 per cent certain that Gareth Gates was robbed.

You can still remember when floppy disks, not USBs, were the removable storage drive of choice.

A WAG is a career path you're seriously considering.

Harry Hill's TV Burp

A TV show about a TV show? That's the kind of television we like! Add that to segments such as *TV Burp Poetry Corner* and *The Knitted Character* and it was a winner.

Skins

Forget the later series – it was all about the wild adventures of Tony and his crew. However, we haven't quite forgiven *Skins* for promising us a teenhood of endless parties, romantic shenanigans and non-stop life-changing revelations.

LITTLE BRITAIN

Yeah but no but yeah. I want that one. I don't like it. The only gay in the village. What a kerfuffle! I'm a lady. Computer says no. Dust, anyone? Need we say any more?

YOU KNOW YOU'RE A CHILD OF THE 2000s WHEN...

You have your **milkshake**, but you're wondering why there are no boys in your yard.

Your first foray into the world of composing was making monotone ringtones on your Nokia.

Your drawers are full of rubber wristbands in aid of charities.

You have zero regrets about your fashion poncho collection.

QUIZ

ONLY A CHILD OF THE 2000s WILL KNOW...

 What was Crazy Frog originally known as?

 After what animal was a famously ugly plastic shoe named?

3 What high-energy dance-based form of exercise became popular in the noughties?

4 What type of fish was Big Mouth Billy?

 Kim Kardashian's stepbrother was featured on which reality show?

LimeWire was used for what?

 Goku, Piccolo and Vegeta are all characters from what series?

8 What was unique about the gel pens everyone went crazy for in the noughties?

YOU KNOW YOU'RE A CHILD OF THE 2000s WHEN...

You practically glued your lips together every time you applied lip gloss.

James Blunt's 'You're Beautiful' is the most romantic song in the world to you.

The biggest falling out of your teen life was when you discovered you weren't in your bestie's top 8 **Myspace** friends.

You are still washing the **hair mascara** out.

The Dark Knight

Batman Begins happened, of course. And we were sort of excited about *The Dark Knight*, sure. But then we saw it and it blew every superhero film we'd ever seen out the water. Christian Bale's husky Batman voice, Heath Ledger's cray Joker — it had the goods.

The Lord of the Rings: The Return of the King

The plot of this film is, as far as we can remember, Legolas surfs an elephant, Gimli can't see and Sam is a boss from start to finish. That and the hundred different endings. It was magnificent and we probably have it to thank for *Game of Thrones*.

Finding Nemo

There are two addresses that I can guarantee you have memorised. One will be your own. And the other will be 42 Wallaby Way, Sydney.

Casino Royale

After the invisible car and Madonna fiasco, it was looking like Bond would never be cool again. When Daniel Craig was cast, we were even more sure of that fact. And yet how wrong we were — gambling, shadowy villains and heartbreaking women. Bond was back.

American Pie

The noughties were prime time for gross-out comedies full of sex and clueless teen boys. None were quite as gross-out and sex-packed as the *American Pie* series (even if there was a touching romantic storyline with Finch and Stifler's mum).

Mean Girls

This. Film. Was. Iconic. It looked like it was going to be just another teen comedy and then turned out to be a quotable, hilarious masterpiece. Hands up if you can perform Kevin G's rap.

YOU KNOW YOU'RE A CHILD OF THE 2000s WHEN...

You spent half of your weekly **pocket money** on pick 'n' mix from Woolworths.

You are a card-carrying member
of either **Team Edward** or
Team Jacob.

Your parents didn't let you get a
Mohawk so you compromised
with a fauxhawk.

There wasn't a hairstyle that
wasn't improved by adding
a **mini-quiff**.

QUIZ

ONLY A CHILD OF THE 2000s WILL KNOW...

1. Jamie Oliver became the face of which supermarket?

2. Outrageous Original and Cool Cola are both flavours of what chewing gum?

3. In 2006 Nestlé caused a minor panic among children when they did what to Smarties?

4. What flavours did Cadbury Snaps come in?

5 Which special Doritos range was discontinued in 2005?

6 What was the best way to cook McCain Microchips?

7 In 2002–2003, which food-based Government health initiative was introduced?

8 What was the name of Cadbury's white chocolate bar?

YOU KNOW YOU'RE A CHILD OF THE 2000s WHEN...

You still believe you can *wingardium leviosa* objects towards you when you're feeling lazy.

You were twelve and owned more **pashminas** than your nan.

You thought your **mismatched earrings** were the height of quirky fashion.

You can only say the word '**donkey**' in a Scottish accent.

Popped-collar polos

Looking back, it isn't clear why we thought wearing our collars up around our ears was such a great idea. Perhaps it was to look bigger to predators and rivals. Perhaps we were just really ashamed of our necks. Either way those collars had to be popped.

Cardigans

In a trend our grandad was happy to see return, menswear was all about the cardigan. No longer was the humble cardie a sure-fire sign that you were a massive nerd; now it was the cool kids who wore them.

HOODIES UNDER BLAZERS

The noughties were all about looks that were formal yet informal. If they could be summed up in a clothing style then they would be 'smart cas'. We reached peak smart cas with the ultimate clash of office-wear and comfort: the hoodie worn under the blazer.

YOU KNOW YOU'RE A CHILD OF THE 2000s WHEN...

Everything you said was carefully planned to be as 'random' as possible.

Your journey into the world of music started with **Good Charlotte** and **My Chemical Romance**.

You and your friends sustained more than a few **injuries** trying your own *Jackass* stunts.

You diligently practised your best **bullet-dodging** technique, à la *The Matrix*.

QUIZ

ONLY A CHILD OF THE 2000s WILL KNOW...

 1 How long was Britney Spears married to her childhood sweetheart for?

2 Janet Jackson lost part of her costume during a Super Bowl performance, showing which body part?

 3 Who was the highest-paid actress of the noughties?

In a 2005 interview with Oprah Winfrey, what did Tom Cruise famously do while expressing his love for new girlfriend Katie Holmes?

 In 2009 Kanye West's infamous interruption of Taylor Swift at the MTV Video Music Awards turned into what meme?

 Teen sweethearts Zac Efron and Vanessa Hudgens met on the set of which Disney film?

 In 2001 Winona Ryder was caught committing what illegal act?

 What was the name of the 'villain' of Channel 4's first series of *Big Brother*?

YOU KNOW YOU'RE A CHILD OF THE 2000s WHEN...

Eyeliner companies hadn't done such a roaring trade since the sixties.

You pulled your hair into such a **tight ponytail**, you looked years younger (practically single figures).

You would use **highlighter** and tippex to give yourself a funky manicure.

You determined how cool you were by how many **buckles** you had on your pirate boots.

Skinny jeans

Ah skinny jeans, those glorious leg-numbing fashion items. We all heard the stories about a friend of a friend of a friend who had to be cut out of her jeans by the fire service and rushed to hospital, but it was never enough to deter us from squeezing into our skinnies.

Hippie dresses over flared jeans

One of those 'styles' it's better to forget. The jeans were meant to add some 'edge' to those floaty, floral dresses, but looking at the photos they seem to just add 'doesn't know how to dress herself' vibes.

Blazers

These were almost always paired with skinnies and the straightest hair ever, creating a look so sleek it must have been aerodynamic.

Denim miniskirts

The beloved denim skirt's hemline rose throughout the noughties until it was essentially just a denim belt — with glamour model Jodie Marsh actually wearing a belt on several occasions.

Ugg boots

The most expensive pair of outdoor slippers ever to be made, these babies had us begging relatives who were holidaying abroad to chuck all their clothes and just fill their suitcases with Ugg boots to bring back for us. Most commonly seen paired with...

Juicy Couture velour tracksuits

OK, so maybe we didn't look very stylish, but we were definitely comfortable. Still, better not to remember that time we all went around with 'juicy' branded across our bums.

YOU KNOW YOU'RE A CHILD OF THE 2000s WHEN...

You spent more on **flavoured lip balms** than on sweets.

You did virtually no exercise
but still always wore
chequered sweatbands.

You had to throw out all
your baseball caps and buy
trucker caps.

You thought a tie and
T-shirt was the ultimate in
cutting-edge fashion.

QUIZ

ONLY A CHILD OF THE 2000s WILL KNOW...

 In which year did the Apple iPhone first hit stores?

 Which all-time bestselling console was released in 2000?

 This iconic noughties video game has become the bestselling game of all time. What was it?

 In what year did the iTunes Music Store launch?

5 What was Facebook's original name?

 6 What was Motorola's bestselling flip phone called?

 7 In 2005 MSN Messenger was rebranded as what?

8 In which year did Dyson release its mind-blowing new hand dryer, the Airblade?

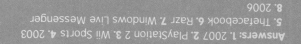

YOU KNOW YOU'RE A CHILD OF THE 2000s WHEN...

Your mum had to help you out of your **skinny jeans** at least once.

Your fringe was permanently plastered to one side of your face.

You owned a keffiyeh scarf in every colour.

You know for sure that Heath Ledger's Joker is the best Joker.

Chunky highlights

Bye bye subtle dye job, hello wearing your highlights as a badge of pride. The aim wasn't to look natural – the aim was to assert your dominance by having as many different colours, in the widest swathes possible, plastered all over your head.

Spiked hair

While girls were aiming for a 'camo' effect with their hair, guys were rocking some electric shock chic with their hair. It could be gelled straight up, it could be gelled to the side, it could be gelled in every direction – but it had to be gelled!

BIEBER HAIR

Whether you were an emo or a Belieber, your hairstyle was the same. The only downside: your grandparents wouldn't stop making lame jokes about you not being able to see with all that hair in your eyes.

YOU KNOW YOU'RE A CHILD OF THE 2000s WHEN...

Your parents have never forgiven you for lying about exactly what happens in a *Grand Theft Auto* game.

Family Guy and *South Park* sessions with your friends were a must.

If you could have an ironic children's cartoon pencil case for work, you totes would.

You still use the phrase 'totes'.

QUIZ

ONLY A CHILD OF THE 2000s WILL KNOW...

1. In which year did the Queen Mother turn 100?

2. How many terms did George W. Bush serve as president of the United States?

3. How many seasons did *Friends* run for before ending in 2004?

4. Who won the first series of *Pop Idol*?

5 What was the name of the device used to record films and TV shows before DVDs?

6 What form of exercise did the 118 118 characters take part in during the original adverts?

7 In what year did Pluto get declassified from planet to dwarf planet?

8 Which chart music TV programme was aired for the last time in 2006?

Answers: 1. 2000 **2.** Two **3.** Ten **4.** Will Young **5.** VCR **6.** Running **7.** 2006 **8.** Top of the Pops

YOU KNOW YOU'RE A CHILD OF THE 2000s WHEN...

You're still not completely clear on what the Millennium Bug was.

You feel guilty because you've still not read *White Teeth* (even though you pretend you have).

You own an unworn pair of gold hot pants, à la Kylie.

You remember when Freddos cost ten pence.

'Hey Ya!' by OutKast

OutKast are some sort of wizards because every time we hear this song we *still* automatically stretch out our arms and wiggle our fingers and then shake it much in the manner of a Polaroid picture. It's like we can't help ourselves.

'Dry Your Eyes' by The Streets

After hilarious hits such as 'Fit But You Know It', we weren't aware that The Streets had such potential for emotion. If you visit the YouTube page for this song you'll find people still posting emotional comments about this song. D'awww.

'Last Nite' by The Strokes

All it takes is this song to come on at the club and you find yourself with your arms wrapped around strangers, jumping up and down like an utter madman.

'Welcome to the Black Parade' by My Chemical Romance

Take yourself back to the times when you only wanted to wear clothes that were black and decorated with skulls, when you brushed your hair over one eye and declared *this isn't a phase, Mum*. Oh yes, I'm talking about the My Chemical Romance days. I'm sorry to remind you.

'Feel Good Inc.' by Gorillaz

We didn't know quite what to make of this song when it first came out and yet within a few listens we couldn't get that hook out of our heads.

'I Kissed a Girl' by Katy Perry

It seems a bit tame nowadays, but at the time 'I Kissed a Girl' caused quite the scandal! Bless, we were so much more innocent in those days.

**YOU KNOW YOU'RE
A CHILD OF THE
2000s
WHEN...**

You still get the David Brent
dance out at Christmas parties
and you still think it's funny.

You recall having to type your
emojis out by hand.

You're fluent in **Baltimore** slang,
thanks to *The Wire*.

You sort of still fancy
Robbie Williams.

QUIZ

ONLY A CHILD OF THE 2000s WILL KNOW...

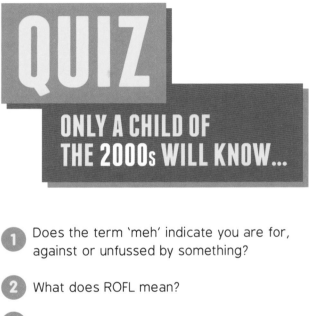

1. Does the term 'meh' indicate you are for, against or unfussed by something?

2. What does ROFL mean?

3. What is a bromance?

4. Pwned and 1337 are words from what language?

5) A slang term for an older woman seeking romantic relationships with younger men became popular. What is it?

6) Glamping is an offshoot of which activity?

7) What satirical TV show spawned the popular use of the word 'omnishambles'?

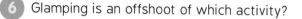

YOU KNOW YOU'RE A CHILD OF THE 2000s WHEN...

You're sort of glad that documentaries aren't such a 'thing' any more, no offence Michael Moore.

You know where you were when
'Crazy in Love' dropped.

You had your own graffiti 'street
name' for a while and tried to
make your mum call you by it.

You haven't worked out whether
The Da Vinci Code was real
or made up.

MILF

Thank you *American Pie* for that charming phrase. We lived in fear that someone would refer to our mother using that word — gross.

Chillin'

Was 'Wot u up 2?' 'Chillin'' the most texted conversation of the noughties? Possibly. Not up to much? You were chillin'. Out and about? You were chillin'. Doing literally anything at any time? Chillin'.

Fetch

Stop trying to make 'fetch' happen, Gretchen.

TEXT SPEAK

How r u? Gr8. LOL. For a moment it seemed like we had revolutionised language forever, so how come we're back to using full words? Oh yes, smartphones. I suppose that the ability to access music, films, the internet and a whole world of apps makes up for the loss of utterly unintelligible language.

YOU KNOW YOU'RE A CHILD OF THE 2000s WHEN...

Your first foray into naughty internet content was Belle de Jour's blog.

You have an abandoned **blog** of your own somewhere.

You remember **Russell Brand** before he became all respectable and had a baby.

You still have nightmares about **Andrew Lloyd Webber** thanks to *Any Dream Will Do.*

QUIZ

ONLY A CHILD OF THE 2000s WILL KNOW...

 1 Which animal had been let out in the Baha Men's hit single?

 2 'The Rock Show' was a single from which Blink 182 album?

 **3** Which rapper featured on Beyoncé's single, 'Crazy in Love'?

 4 Which band, whose breakthrough single was 'Harder to Breathe', was originally called Kara's Flowers?

Name the two members of OutKast.

 In which year was The Street's 'When You Wasn't Famous' released?

 What activity was taking place in the video for Eric Prydz's single 'Call on Me'?

 What was the name of Gnarls Barkley's breakthrough single?

YOU KNOW YOU'RE A CHILD OF THE **2000s** WHEN...

Your introduction to opera was from *Jerry Springer: The Opera*. Who said you weren't cultured?

You snuck in to the first **Saw** film.

You know that **the Doctor** and Rose were meant to be.

... And you see what your parents were banging on about with the **Daleks**.

Blink-182

For some noughties kids, Blink weren't just a band — they were a lifestyle. Combined with a mostly unused skateboard under one arm, Dickies shorts and long socks and a healthy diet of *Jackass*, Blink-182 were all you needed.

Robbie Williams

Oh, that cheeky chappie, king of our hearts (and our mum's hearts). For the first half of the noughties he was everywhere, even duetting with Nicole frickin' Kidman! Who could have predicted that Take That would one day rise again and be more popular than him?

Arctic Monkeys

Amongst all the military jackets and shoe-gazing poetry of the Indie movement came one thunderous, game-changing single. 'I Bet You Look Good on the Dancefloor' blew everyone away, and Arctic Monkeys have been great ever since.

Amy Winehouse

Oh, Amy. With her big beehive and bigger voice, she blew our minds with her retro-modern sound and catchy hooks. She paved the way for the powerhouse that is Adele.

Lady Gaga

Paws up, Little Monsters! Lady Gaga came seemingly from nowhere in the late noughties, bringing the weird and wonderful back into fashion (and leading us to attempt an awful lot of arts and crafts with our hair).

YOU KNOW YOU'RE A CHILD OF THE **2000s** WHEN...

You thought *Guitar Hero* would turn you into a superstar guitarist.

Your mum took you to see *Billy Elliot* and... it wasn't bad actually.

You first became aware of extreme weather with **Hurricane Katrina**.

You wanted to become a wildlife camera person after seeing *Planet Earth*.

QUIZ

ONLY A CHILD OF THE 2000s WILL KNOW...

1 What was the 'Bieber' haircut?

2 What was the name of Amy Winehouse's famous, stacked hairstyle?

3 Long, contrasting extensions were popular in the noughties. What colour(s) was Christina Aguilera's hair in the video for 'Dirrty'?

4 What was the nickname for Victoria Beckham's famous angled bob?

Which brand of straightener became the ultimate hair accessory?

 Hair colour that came in tubes with an applicator was called what?

 Which Elvis-inspired hairstyle was warn with many a ponytail in the noughties?

 The ideal noughties highlight was: a) thin or b) chunky?

YOU KNOW YOU'RE A CHILD OF THE 2000s WHEN...

You can still be persuaded to partake in a game of **bogies**.

You still have nightmares about *Grizzly Tales for Gruesome Kids*.

You've still not recovered from *Friends* ending.

Your parents still suspect you've been irrevocably warped by signals from your mobile phone.

YouTube

YouTube was launched in 2005 and with it went all of our spare time. Let's go way back and remember some golden oldies: *Star Wars* kid, Kelly and her shoes, Auto-Tune the News. And you can't forget that classic, Charlie bit my finger! Oh Charlie, you scamp.

Facebook

Remember when you spent hours a day poking people on Facebook and your grandparents didn't even know what it was, let alone had a cute couples' account on it? When you spent time topping up your Facebook aquarium and had to get really creative with how you wrote statuses because of the strange format? Ah, us too.

BARACK OBAMA

It was 2008 and America had just elected some kind of superhero. Or at least that's the impression that we got, what with all the posters, the rejoicing — oh yes, and the Nobel peace prize. No pressure Barack, no pressure at all.

YOU KNOW YOU'RE A CHILD OF THE 2000s WHEN...

You're still collecting the pieces of your tiny mind after reading *The God Delusion*.

You spent the entire decade preparing for the **Digital Switchover**, which you thought would be a teensy bit more dramatic than it eventually was.

You know that **prank calls** can get you fired, à la Wossy and Russell Brand.

You still think *Slumdog Millionaire* is the greatest love story ever told.

QUIZ

ONLY A CHILD OF THE 2000s WILL KNOW...

1. Sienna Miller was credited with popularising what style of fashion?

2. After they moved on from acting, mega-rich twins Mary-Kate and Ashley created which fashion house?

3. What was the name of the jeans with waistlines that were more hipline?

4. Celebrities popularised which brand of velour tracksuit?

5 What sleeveless upper-body garment was wildly popular and often worn without a shirt?

6 What was the optimum length of a cardigan?

7 What was the name of the brand of comfortable boot that originated in Australia?

8 Which hat in the flat-cap family was popular in the noughties?

YOU KNOW YOU'RE A CHILD OF THE 2000s WHEN...

You thought you'd be buried in your **Dickies** shorts.

You had a sneaky google of 'Is it OK to be attracted to blue giants?' after watching *Avatar*.

You've suppressed all memories of the lame under-eighteens club nights you went to.

You're anxiously waiting for the arthritis you were meant to get from all the finger snapping you did.

Nintendo DS

Sorry, PlayStation Portable, but we're team *Zelda* and *Phoenix Wright: Ace Attorney* until we die. Represent.

Nintendo Wii / Wii Fit

Finally! A healthy video game that got our parents off our backs about playing too much. Except... we couldn't get *them* off the console. No fair, Dad, how am I meant to become a tennis pro like this?

Motorola Razr

Sorry, Nokia — the Razr was everything. Though we may have broken the odd one or two by swinging it open too wildly.

Baby-G watches

We would NEVER take our Baby-G off, to the point that the straps would sometimes fall off our wrists through wear, tear and maybe the tiniest bit of mildew.

Webcams

Oh, webcams. So many regrets. So many things filmed that can never be unfilmed. So much blackmail material held by our friends.

iPod products

The adverts were cool, but the gadgets were even cooler. At first our minds were blown by the fact that we didn't have to carry our CDs everywhere any more, then suddenly you could shake your iPod to shuffle it, view cover art and even watch films. The future. It was here.

YOU KNOW YOU'RE A CHILD OF THE 2000s WHEN...

You have burnt all photos of a time when it was cool to wear **low-rise jeans** with your thong on show.

You received **endless belts** for Christmas from your dad, who thought he was making a hilarious joke about your jeans-wearing habits.

You devoured *A Series of Unfortunate Events* during your 'edgy' phase.

You still cringe about that time you changed your Facebook **relationship status** to 'it's complicated'.

QUIZ

ONLY A CHILD OF THE 2000s WILL KNOW...

 What was the preferred manner of wearing your shirt collar?

 Complete the name of this trucker hat brand: Von _____

 What was the nickname for the popular imitation-mohawk hairstyle?

 What was the preferred colour for trainers?

5 What was the nickname of the small goatee fashionable in the noughties?

 6 What was the name of the shell used in the fashionable chokers of the time?

7 This Palestinian chequered scarf was worn by mildly rebellious teens everywhere. What was it called?

8 Which athletic fashion line is known by the initials A and F?

YOU KNOW YOU'RE A CHILD OF THE 2000s WHEN...

Dido's 'White Flag' is your
anthem for your favourite
relationship 'pairing'.

You've yet to throw out
your extensive collection of
phone charms.

You spent hours finding the
perfect dramatic-but-subtle song
lyrics for your **MSN name**.

You regret never making it as a
'**Myspace celebrity**'.

Celebrity name abbreviations

LiLo, J-Lo, Xtina; it seems like we really gave up on writing anything out in full during the noughties. And don't get us started on the couple names. RIP TomKat and your sofa-bouncing ways. RIP Bennifer and all your fake tan. Sniff, RIP Brangelina, we thought you were going to make it!

Orlando Bloom

Reluctant pirate, badass elf, possessor of great hair. Orlando was the noughties teen heart-throb. Just call us Mrs Legolas Turner.

PARIS HILTON

The term 'celebrity' became a bit of a looser definition, with the wildly popular reality TV genre coming to the forefront in the 2000s. Over all your Spencers and your Audrinas reigned Paris, our dog-toting reality princess.

YOU KNOW YOU'RE A CHILD OF THE 2000s WHEN...

This **big eyebrow trend** is against everything you've ever stood for.

You're still hoping **Ozzy Osbourne** will adopt you. Or maybe you can adopt him.

You had to change your **email address** from mentalhamster@ awesomemail.com.

If you bump into friends in the street you shout, 'You shall not pass!'

QUIZ

 Who voiced Dory, the regal tang fish with short-term memory loss in *Finding Nemo*?

 Slumdog Millionaire is structured around the Indian version of which British game show?

 In *Spider-Man*, starring Tobey Maguire, the main villain was known by which pseudonym?

 The eponymous main character of *Borat* is from which country?

5 Teen comedy *Mean Girls* was written by which comedian?

 6 What is Napoleon Dynamite's favourite animal?

7 Who curses Sophie in *Howl's Moving Castle*?

8 In what year was the final *The Lord of the Rings* film, *The Return of the King*, released?

YOU KNOW YOU'RE A CHILD OF THE 2000s WHEN...

Wearing your **studded belt** off-centre means you're cool.

You found all your cheat codes
on a piece of paper the other day.

If asked to, you absolutely could
write 'boobs' on a calculator.

You still hold all your parties at
Laser Quest.

Bertie Bott's Every Flavour Beans

We had some real questions about these treats when they came out. Would we really have to eat earwax- and vomit-flavoured beans? And the answer was... yes.

Cupcakes

No longer were cupcakes the province of every child's party but the new ultra-cool foodstuff. Celebs were seen toting boxes of them around (like they actually ate them) and we found ourselves spending triple the amount of pocket money than usual just to bag these sugary delights.

Goodbye fast food

All noughties children are bonded by their survival of The Great Fast Food Purge, as everyone suddenly became super-health-conscious. Thanks *Supersize Me*, thanks Jamie Oliver. Thanks a bunch.

Energy drinks

If we couldn't have Maccy D's, we could at least have Red Bull and Monster. Energy drinks were kind of healthy, right? Right?

Flavoured Coke

Lime Coke, Vanilla Coke, Cherry Coke — we went mad for Coke with even more sugar added. And then we went mad afterwards, from all that sugar. Happy days spent bouncing off the wall.

No-Carbs / Atkins

It was a little early for diets for us but Mum sure had some strange-looking dinners for a while. Still, not as strange as that time Beyoncé drank only maple syrup water to lose weight.

YOU KNOW YOU'RE A CHILD OF THE 2000s WHEN...

You have a copy of *Captain Underpants* tucked into the literary classic you're pretending to read.

You may have hospitalised someone just by passing them while wearing a whole can of **Lynx** body spray.

You made meticulously planned, ultimately **crap playlists** to burn onto a CD.

You retook your Harry Potter **Sorting Hat** test until you were in the 'right' house.

QUIZ

 1. What was the name of the ginger, winking host of game show *The Weakest Link*?

 2. *Jamie's School Dinners* famously knocked which tasty treat off school menus everywhere?

 3. Name two of the original teens from the first series of *Skins*.

 4. What channel did comedy show *Little Britain* initially appear on?

5 What was the address of *Desperate Housewives* Susan, Lynette, Bree and Gabrielle?

6 How long would the wives on *Wife Swap* swap families?

7 Lacey Chabert passed the voice acting role of Meg from *Family Guy* to which actress?

8 Which TV channel did *My Super Sweet 16* air on?

YOU KNOW YOU'RE A CHILD OF THE 2000s WHEN...

You performed for more people than you'd care to admit on your VJ Starz Video Karaoke Machine.

You're scarred from all the times you tripped on the cloth strips on your cargo pants.

You're still not over the discrepancy between Hermione's Yule Ball dress in the book and in the film.

You're secretly grateful that scarves are a normal width again.

Tammy Girl

There was one reason and one reason only to accept going shopping with your mum. If you suffered through the trauma of Marks and Sparks and Clarks then you could go to heaven on earth... Tammy Girl.

Livestrong wristbands

As the mid-noughties hit, suddenly we all became philanthropists and campaigned for all sorts of charities. Or at least we bought the wristbands. We were so deep.

MSN MESSENGER

Friendships lived and died on MSN. You could go home from school one day best of pals and the next it was all-out war, just through a misinterpreted message or delayed reply on Messenger. Such heady days.

YOU KNOW YOU'RE A CHILD OF THE 2000s WHEN...

You have to hold yourself back from giving your work the **WordArt** treatment.

You have a fave
Bedingfield sibling.

You're not French but you sure
do have a large collection
of **berets**.

You still sort of like
The Phantom Menace.

1. SpongeBob SquarePants lived in a pineapple under the sea, but what was his town called?

2. *Lizzie McGuire* starred which noughties teen celebrity?

3. You gained more time in the final round of *Jungle Run* by collecting statues of which animal?

4. What were the names of the Powerpuff Girls?

What colours were Cosmo and Wanda's hair in *The Fairly OddParents*?

 William, the ghost in *The Ghost Hunter*, was a shoeshine boy from which era?

 What was the name of Mona's pet cat in *Mona the Vampire*?

 In *Dick and Dom in da Bungalow*, what was Creamy Muck Muck?

Answers: 1. Bikini Bottom **2.** Hilary Duff **3.** Monkeys **4.** Bubbles, Blossom and Buttercup **5.** Pink and green **6.** The Victorian era **7.** Fang **8.** Custard

121

YOU KNOW YOU'RE A CHILD OF THE 2000s WHEN...

You serve your best Blue Steel any time you look in the mirror.

You attended a few therapy sessions after trying vanilla-ice-cream-flavoured **Monster Munch**.

You're still waiting for that **Hogwarts** letter.

You think *Elf* is the ultimate Christmas film.

Wayne Rooney

After the glory of Beckham it was hard getting our heads around a footballer that wasn't exactly perfectly groomed and devastatingly handsome. Poor Rooney — it's not enough that he's a shockingly good footballer; the UK can never forgive him for looking a bit like a potato.

Usain Bolt

Are there any words to describe the feeling of seeing the world's fastest man smash the record for being fast? Add the cheeky little celly at the end and he smashed our hearts too. What a time to be alive.

Roger Federer

If you want to know who won Wimbledon in the 2000s, then the answer is essentially 'Federer'.

He had his breakthrough in 2003 and then he did it again. And again. And didn't stop doing it until 2008, when Nadal thwarted his attempt to beat Björn Borg's record five-straight Wimbledon wins.

The Williams Sisters

If you want to know who won *everything* in women's tennis, that would be the Williams sisters. In 2002 they occupied the first and second spot in the rankings and by 2009 they... still occupied the first and second spot in the rankings (with a few ups and downs in between).

Lewis Hamilton

Sorry Jenson Button, but it had been a bit of a sad time for UK motorsports until Lewis Hamilton swept Formula1 in 2008. He was cool, he was fast and he was record-breaking, and he gave British F1 fans something to be excited about.

YOU KNOW YOU'RE A CHILD OF THE 2000s WHEN...

You remember when there was no **send receipt** on phones and 'I'm sorry, I didn't see the message' was a valid excuse.

You had to watch
Everybody Loves Raymond
when you were off sick.

You still hold a moment of silence
for Marissa Cooper.

You don't wish people 'Merry
Christmas' — you hope they have a
'Proper crimbo'.

If you're interested in finding out more
about our books, find us on Facebook at
Summersdale Publishers and follow us on
Twitter at **@Summersdale**.

www.summersdale.com